# THE FOUNDR

# modo®

## NOTES

# ESSENTIAL modo® 3D GRAPHICS TECHNIQUES FOR ADVANCED BEGINNERS

## MODELING · IMAGE MAPS · LIGHTING · RIGGING

**Ken Freed**

**Visit us at www.kenfreedsoftware.com**

**CCB Publishing**

**British Columbia, Canada**

The Foundry modo® Notes:
Essential modo® 3D Graphics Techniques for Advanced Beginners
ISBN-13 978-1-77143-149-1
First Edition

Library and Archives Canada Cataloguing in Publication
Freed, Ken, 1954-, author
The foundry modo® notes: essential modo® 3D graphics techniques for
advanced beginners / by Ken Freed. -- First edition.
ISBN 978-1-77143-149-1 (pbk.)
Additional cataloguing data available from Library and Archives Canada

Publisher: CCB Publishing
        British Columbia, Canada
        www.ccbpublishing.com

# CONTENTS

# INTRODUCTION

Before we begin, I have a confession to make:

## I am not a modo® expert!

- Since I do not use The Foundry (formerly Luxology) modo® full time, I frequently refer to my notes. That's why in fact, I collected my notes and wrote this book - for occasional users like myself, with moderate experience, who have similar needs.

- I have put a fair amount of time into learning modo®, and can usually create (or figure out how to create) what I need. I truly envy those who are more skilled at using modo® than me - and can do more impressive work (animation, lighting, texturing, particle and volumetric effects, rigging) than I can (and/or do it faster than I can). Most of the people I correspond with on the forums are forever discovering new aspects of modo® - even after several years of use. It's my impression that very few have a complete knowledge of modo®.

This book has been written for the occasional to frequent modo® user and is meant to be both a quick training guide and a reference/refresher. Prior to writing this book, I was told (by good and sincere people) that to market a modo® book, I had to present the user with at least a simple project, so that they would get quick results. I have found that most modo® books and (especially) tutorials teach by illustrating how to do this or that project - which imparts more of a "paint by numbers" approach to learning modo® than an understanding of repeatedly used underlying basics. Trying to learn modo® from most video tutorials in this manner is like trying to learn a foreign language without first learning some basic vocabulary and grammar; i.e. it's the difference between using stock phrases vs. being able to express an idea. This book distills out a set of high usage modo® vocabulary and grammar in a "high information density" style (including plenty of screen shots), so that you can quickly get (back) into using the software, and more easily follow tutorials. It uses PC key nomenclature and the modo® 601 screens to illustrate various operations.

In an ideal world, many sequences of operations (like importing a backdrop image, or creating a UV map) would be reduced to a single button push - but alas - this would cut down on the overall generality of the software for the sake of beginners. Keeping in mind that 3D graphics software is NOT as intuitive as Microsoft Word® or PowerPoint®, just realizing/remembering where things are and what (sometimes disparate) parts of the screen relate to others (along with when additional mouse clicks and/or keystrokes are sometimes necessary) is often half the challenge for the advanced modo® beginner.

# STARTING A NEW SCENE

## Reading In a modo® LXO File

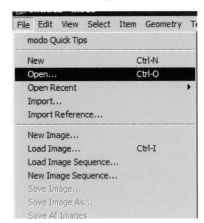

IMPORTANT: While the artwork is saved, the accompanying modo® SETUP is NOT saved.

- E.G., If you saved with a perspective view, and you read your .lxo artwork file back in on (e.g.) a front view and a different magnification, then you will see the artwork on that latest front view and magnification setup.

IMPORTANT: After you read in a file, you will (most likely) have to reselect the mesh layer under the Item list (in the upper right) to continue editing your mesh.

- If not, your mesh will "seem" uneditable.

## Resetting The Screen Before Starting

As stated above, upon starting modo®, the screen state remains where you left it the last time you used the software. Especially for a beginner (who does not always hit the right keys), this can be problematic - since the screen can get all messed up (axis cocked, mesh at an awkward angle,...). This section tells you how to straighten it out.

> A key: Fit all (in the viewport)
>
> O key: Visibility options popup

### *MUST DOs EVERY TIME YOU START modo®:*

**1) Fit and align the Viewport.**

As illustrated on the right:

The A key (Fit All) is handy for quickly situating your mesh in the viewport.

- If you use the O key and check "Show Lights" and "Show Cameras", the A key will zoom out so that you can see these too.

**2) Rotate the Viewport so that the Y axis (in the lower left) is pointing upward, the X axis points to the right and the Z axis is coming out towards you.**

- An upward Y axis is usually the default "up vector" for rigging.

- Many tutorials assume symmetry along the X axis (i.e., the right and left sides of the object mirror each other at the X=0 parting line).

## OPTIONAL:

3) (Assuming your graphics card supports OpenGL) set to the (Perspective, Advanced OpenGL, Ray GL:OFF) settings in the upper left corner of the viewport.

> END key: Reset the Workplane
>
> Q key, spacebar: Drops a tool (spacebar also rotates through vertices,edges,polygon selection)
>
> ESC key: Drops a constraint.

4) Make sure that all Action Center and Falloff options are unchecked. Make sure Snapping is off.

5) Reset the Workplane.
- The END key will also do this.

6) Other resets:
- Q or Spacebar (to drop a tool).
- ESC key (to drop a constraint).

# Screen Problems & Solutions

**OCCASIONAL PROBLEM:** If the screen is still messed up, File -> Reset (shown on the left) will reset modo® to the preferences:

The Preferences that modo® resets to are found under
        System -> Preferences.

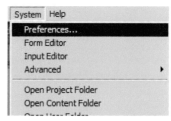

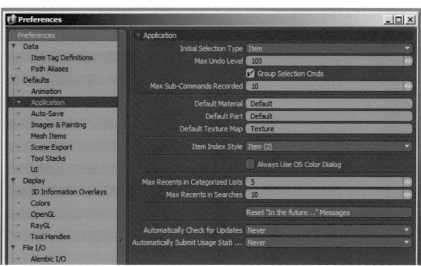

After using the previous File -> Reset, hit the O key and reset "Show Centers" dropdown to:
Show Centers [Selected] .

- File->Reset sets this to [None].

**OCCASIONAL PROBLEM:** If you cannot see the handles for the (move, rotate, etc.) manipulators, reset it by selecting the (move, rotate, etc.) manipulator and go to:

View menu->Tool Handles->Draw Style

and reset it to "Basic".

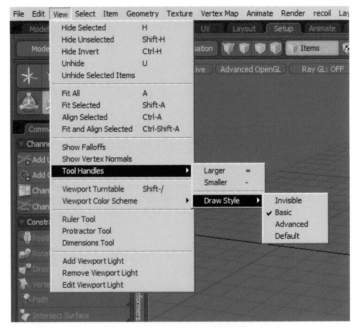

**RARE PROBLEM:** If some other screen layout appears reset it via:

Layout menu->Layouts->601 Default Layout.

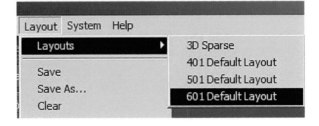

# MODELING

## Creating New Item Layers

N key: Create new Item layer

CNTRL-D: to duplicate one Item layer onto another (new) Item layer

The Items list shows the layers which contain polygon meshes.

The N key is the same as the menu driven: Add Item -> Mesh (in the upper right by the Item List).

Right mouse clicking on the layer will let you rename it.

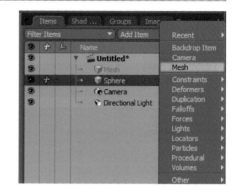

INFO: (Unlike Photoshop® layers) The order in which Item layers are stacked (under the Item tab in the upper right) only matters with background constraints (where the constraining/background layer must be ABOVE the layer being constrained).

The order of the Shader Tree layers (which will be covered later under materials & lighting) DOES matter. The materials toward the top override those below them.

CNTRL-D : Use this to duplicate an Item selected mesh on one mesh layer into another mesh layer.

- Caution: watch out for where the <u>center</u> of the copied mesh winds up. You might have to move the center - especially if you only selected part of the original mesh to copy.

  - The center on the new mesh stays where it was relative to the larger original mesh - hence copying a wheel from a car might keep the center of the wheel off to the side on the new mesh (where the original center of the car was on the old mesh).

# Putting A New Shape Into The Viewport

## In this example we will insert a cube.

N key: Create new Item layer

1) Select an empty layer in the Items list (upper right) or hit the N key to make an empty Item layer.

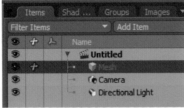

2) Select the Cube.

3) If we (e.g.) want to have nine polygons on each face of the cube, change each of the Segment values to 3 (as shown below). Then hit "APPLY" to apply the new segments.

| Segments X | 3 |
| Y | 3 |
| Z | 3 |

**BIG CONFUSION SOURCE:** Sometimes the shape will get inserted when you hit APPLY, sometimes not. Make sure NONE of the **Size** parameters have gotten (re)set to zero, e.g.:

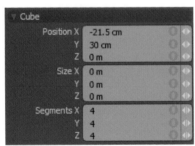

For instance, if you "dragged out a mesh" (as described in the next section) your default position and size parameters on these (cube, sphere, etc.) icons will get changed to those you had at the end of the last drag for that shape.

## Alternatively:

2) Hit SHIFT and click on the cube. This will place the cube in the viewport AND put it in a newly created Item layer.

- The number of segments won't be what you filled out in the Cube properties (in the lower left). They will be those from the time before, so you'll have to tweak the geometry (i.e., add/remove edges to/from the mesh).

## *Dragging Out A Mesh*

Holding down the left mouse button after the (e.g.) cube icon is selected (in the upper left) will allow you to drag out its size in two dimensions in the viewport (via one of the little square handles). After releasing the mouse button you'll get the (little square) scaling handles, along with move (arrow) handles. The spacebar will drop these handles/manipulators.

• Caution: hitting the spacebar a 2nd time might rotate between vertices->edges->polygons selection.

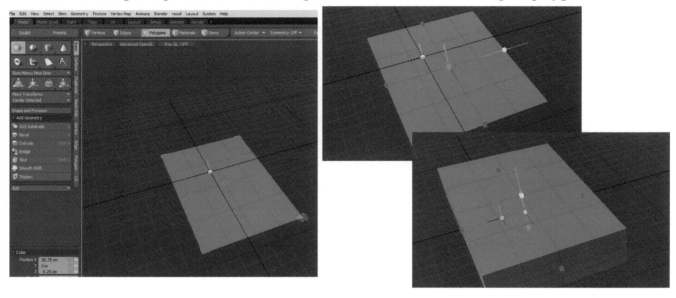

## *Geometry Primitives, Ground Plane, Gear*

Mesh items can also be added via the Geometry menu:

• Note that the plane selected from here cannot be scaled up along the 3rd axis to become a cube.

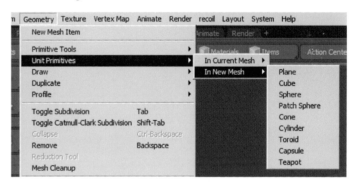

Add Items->Volumes has a built in Ground Plane.

Add Item->Procedural has a built in Gear with various properties.

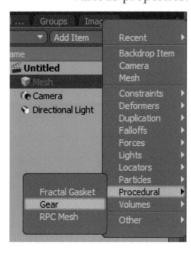

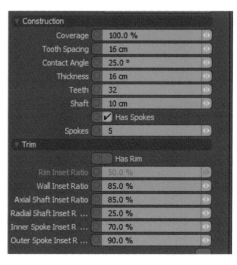

# Starting With A modo® Predefined Mesh

So that you don't have to start with a "primitive" shape/mesh every time you go to model something, modo® has a series of predefined meshes under the Layout tab (just double click or drag the figure into the viewport, then use the A key to center it in the viewport):

Note that (Tab key) subdivisions are in effect for many of these. Selecting the mesh and hitting the Tab key will let you see the non subdivided mesh.

More modo® meshes (and other free assets) are available at the Luxology asset sharing url: http://community/thefoundry.co.uk/asset/.

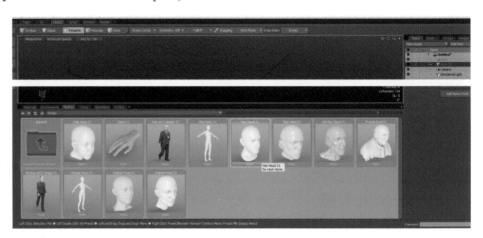

# Instances vs Duplicates

Instance: An instance can be moved, rotated, and scaled independently of its original
    - but -
if the original shape is deformed, the instance will also be deformed.

• Instances save a lot of memory, and are used when you have a lot of copies to make, like (e.g.) rivets on a bridge.

Duplicates: Are completely independent copies of an original.

# Instance Cloning Examples

Some examples of instance cloning (similar options exist for duplicate cloning):

Instance Clone: Tugging on the move handles will give evenly spaced instance clones.

Curve Instance: This might more appropriately be called "Path Instance". Click to set the points of the path, then adjust the Steps (= instances) number in the lower left.

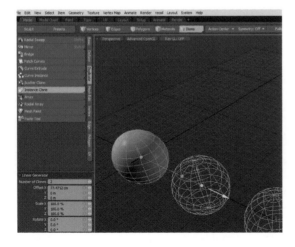

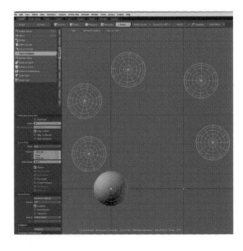

# Selecting Mesh Geometry

L key: Loop select

Cntrl-Left Mouse Click: To unselect a single polygon

SHIFT-UpArrow: To grow a selection

- Holding down the left mouse button and dragging (in Polygon selection mode) will select the polygons that the mouse cursor is dragged over.
- Left mouse button clicking on an edge or vertex will select it.
  - The middle mouse button will select right through the mesh onto the other side.
- Holding the SHIFT key down will let you add to a selection.
- The "[" (left square bracket) key inverts (swaps selected vs non selected) selection on a mesh.

- To deselect a (e.g., mistakenly selected) polygon, use Cntrl-Left Mouse Click (over a polygon, while the other polygons are still selected) .
- Double clicking on a polygon will select all the polygons in its mesh.
- If you cannot select polygons on a shape, it most likely means that shape is on some other Item Layer.

## *Loop Selection*

1) Hold down the Shift key to select two adjacent polygons (sometimes one polygon will be enough, but the loop can then get selected in the wrong direction).

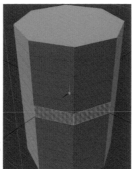

2) Hit the L key to loop select.
- The left and right arrows will move the selected loop up and down along the (e.g.) cylinder.

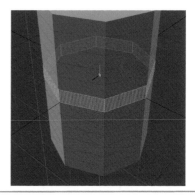

## *Growing A Selection*

Shift-UpArrow:
- To "grow" the selection.

Shift-DownArrow:
- To "shrink" the selection.

Shift-Left/Right Arrow:
- To grow in only one direction.

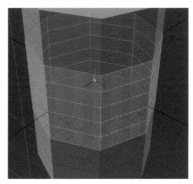

Cntrl-Left Mouse Click (with the mouse cursor over a e.g. polygon) to deselect an individual polygon.

## *Lasso Selection*

Right mouse clicking (in an empty area of the viewport) brings up a popup that includes the Lasso Style selection:

Lasso selection is almost essential for selecting vertices. Right mouse click and drag for lasso selection.

IMPORTANT: Change (from e.g. Advanced OpenGL) to Wire Frame view to select THROUGH (i.e. both sides) of the mesh OR use the middle mouse button, preferably in an orthogonal (front, top, etc.) view to select through the geometry.

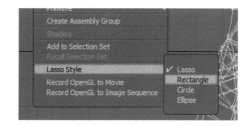

# Move, Rotate, Scale (Manipulators)

| W key: Move a selection |
| E key: Rotate a selection |
| R key: Scale a selection |

Since manipulators get used a LOT, here are the shortcut keys:

- Select what you are Scaling in Polygon Mode (Item mode selections won't scale).

Move    Rotate    Scale

The ALT key presents an alternate set of the above manipulators:

Soft Move    Twist    Taper

These are shortcuts for different types of Linear Falloffs. Use polygon selection with them.

NOTE: You don't move lights with the W key.

- You move them by selecting the light in the Item list, then changing its properties (in the lower right).

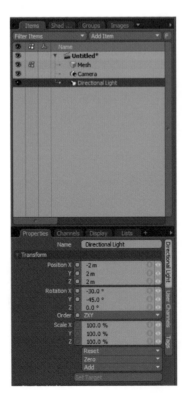

# E

If you want to (e.g.) rotate a mesh 90 degrees, make sure to do it all at once (before deselecting), since the rotational angles (on the left side of the screen) will reset to zero at deselection.

- You have to set the Action Center to Origin if you want to see an absolute rotational value (on the right side of the screen).

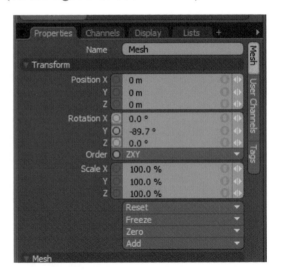

**ADVANCED NOTE:** Components (vertices, edges, polygons) cannot be keyframed (in animation).

- Use (rigging) deformers instead.

# Shaping A Mesh

1) Make a selection (polygons, edges or vertices) on the mesh.
- Drag the mouse across polygons to select them, or
- Right mouse click and Lasso select, or
- Select a polygon and double click (to select the whole mesh).

2) Select a transform or manipulator.

3) Mouse click in the middle of the selected polygons.

4) Select one of the handles which appears and drag, move or deform the mesh.

5) Use the Space Bar to deselect the manipulator..

6) Click off of the mesh in the viewport to deselect the polygons.

## *Extrude, Bevel, Moving, Scaling*

These (often interchangeable) operations are fairly straightforward modo® transforms. Some of their more unusual effects will be summarized here.

### *Thin Walls*

1) Bevel OR Extrude can be used to pull polygons out.
- Note that the Action Center was set to Selection - so that the pull would be done normal to the surface.

2) Then Bevel must be used to "shrink in" the top polygon.

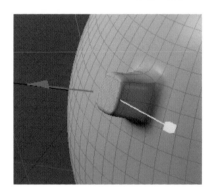

3) Then either Bevel OR Extrude can be used to "push in" and create a thin wall effect.

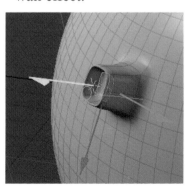

4) The thin wall can then be thickened.

Edge Sliding an edge past the end of a mesh is another way to produce thin wall geometry.

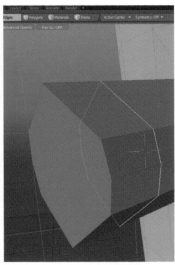

## *Moving*

Moving some vertices on a sphere.

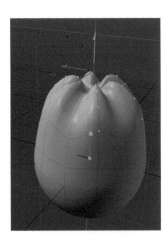

Select an Action Center of Local or Selection to move polygons normal to the surface.

- The most common Action Centers used in tutorials are Origin, Local and none.

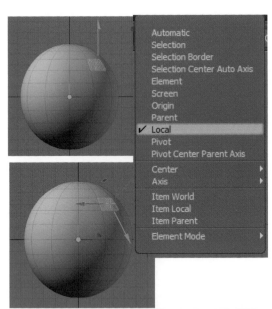

## *Scaling*

Scaling two edges inward (towards the center) on a sphere creates a pear shape.

Note: Scaling out corner edge loops and Beveling out end capping Polygons have similar effects.

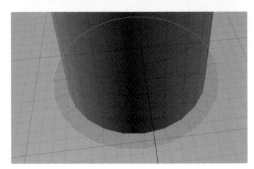

# Flattening A Mesh Selection

Scaling can be used to flatten a surface along an orthogonal plane.

1) Select the vertices to be flattened in wireframe mode, in an orthogonal view (front view shown, with vertices selected for some X value).

2) Adjust the scaling to 0% in the (e.g.) X (lower left) to flatten the vertices.

3) Flattened object in Perspective view (Advanced OpenGL).

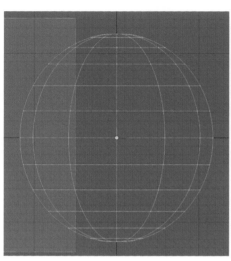

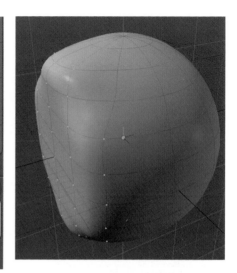

1a) Note you could also hit BACKSPACE to delete the mesh geometry (then select bordering edges and hit the P key to fill in with a polygon), but (when it comes to flattening) this does not always give you what you want.

## Alternative Flattening Method

Note that if your mesh is on the origin and want to flatten to an axis, you can use Set Vertex Position (and set the Vertex Position to zero).

- Depending on how your mesh is sitting, you might have to set the Action Center to Origin first:

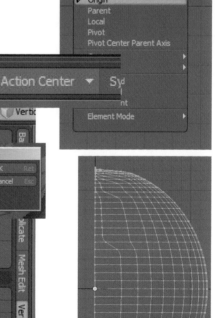

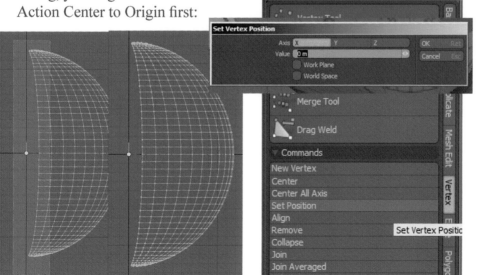

## *Mirroring Along A Parting Line*

Mirroring (or symmetry along the X axis) is used when you have a symmetric model, and only need to model half of it (because you can use mirroring to create the other half).

Assuming you've used one of the previous flattening methods to flatten the mesh along the (e.g.) X=0 parting line, e.g.:

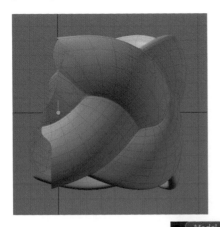 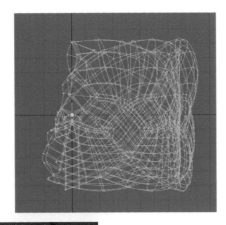 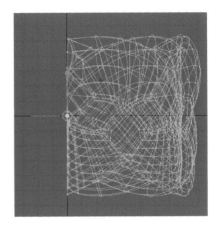

1) Select the whole mesh/item

.

2) Duplicate Mirror.

- Axis X
- Center X = 0

- The mesh will become mirrored across the axis IN ANOTHER LAYER.

3) Cut and paste the mesh from the new layer into the original layer if you want to join the middle edges/parting line.

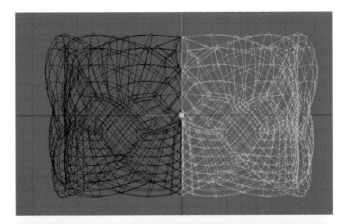

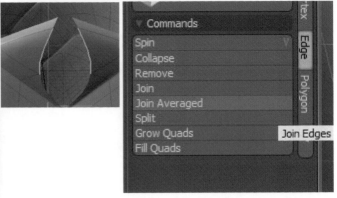

# *Linear Falloffs*

ESC key: Drop falloff tool

ALT key: More basic manipulators

Falloffs vary a manipulator (move, rotate, scale) along a length. They are used for such effects as (e.g.) tapering and bending. For example:

1) Place a cylinder in the viewport and select a manipulator. 2) Apply a Falloff to the manipulator.

3) Align the Falloff to the orthogonal axis. Reverse its direction if needed. The wide end of the Falloff has more manipulator effect and the narrow end has less manipulator effect. There will be no manipulator effect where the Falloff triangle tapers to a point.

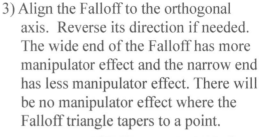

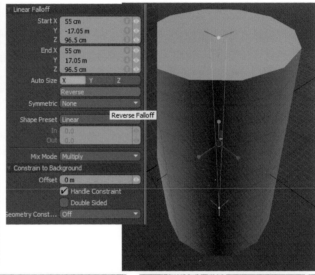

## *Sample Falloffs:*

Radially scaling a cylinder in the <x,z> gives
    "Ease-In"
and
    "Ease-Out"
curves.

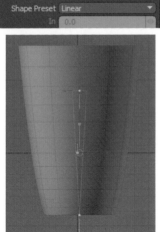

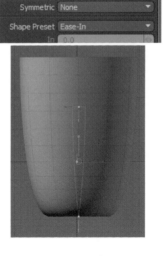

A Falloff with a rotate or move manipulator can also act as a bend:

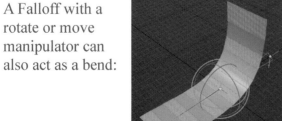

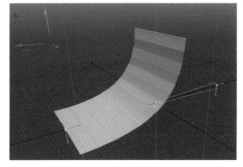

# *Drawing A Closed Shape*

1) Select the curve tool.

2) Turn symmetry on in the X.

3) In an orthogonal (e.g. top) view, draw half the shape (symmetry will draw the other half on the other side of the X axis).

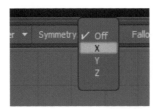

4) Hit the Space Bar to drop the Curve tool.

5) **Turn symmetry off.**

6) Join vertices: In Vertex selection mode, select a vertex. Holding down the Shift Key, select the opposite vertex.

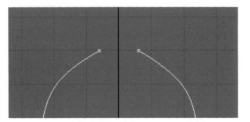

7) Select Join Vertices, then click in the Viewport.

# *Extruding A Profile*

1) Draw a closed shape in the (e.g.) top view as previously described.

2) Change to the Perspective view.

> P key: Close polygon
>
> TAB key: Toggle corner round off
>
> ALT-C: Create more edges across polygons
>
> F9: Render

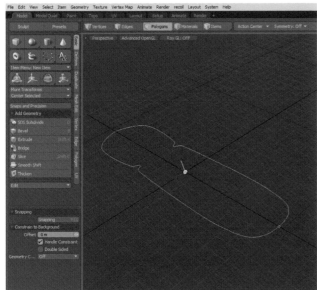

3) Lasso select the closed loop edges **in Polygon mode.**

4) Extrude upward.

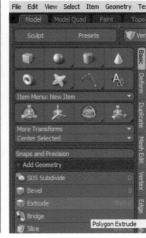 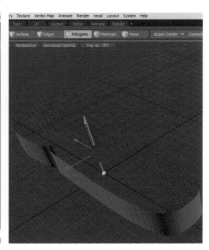

5) Hit the Space Bar to drop the Extrude tool, then (using Edge selection mode and the L key) Loop select the top edge.

6) Hit the P key to close the polygon.

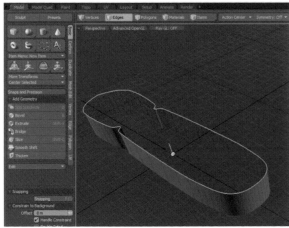 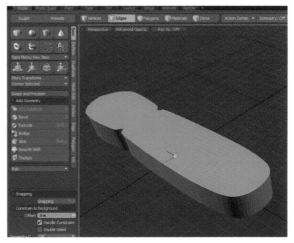

7) Create control edges by beveling in the top polygon slightly, i.e. select the top polygon, hit the B key and bevel in.

8) Loop select the side polygons (i.e. select 2 adjacent polygons, then hit the L key to loop select). Use ALT-C and create two more control edges. Edge slide them towards the top and bottom corners.

9) Select the entire mesh by double clicking on a polygon, then use the Tab key to round off the corners.

10) Change to the Render tab, position the mesh in the camera view, then use F9 to render the image.

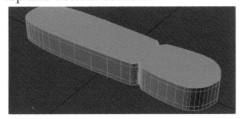 

# *Bend*

1) Select all the polygons by double clicking on a polygon of the mesh.

2) Go to an orthogonal (non perspective) view (e.g. front) to get a neater bend.

3) Select Deform -> Bend.

4) Click on the mesh.

5) Rotate the wheel that appears.

6) Pulling the handle (white crosshairs) can shape the bend as well.

R key: Scale

B key: Bevel

SHIFT key: Hold down to add to the selection

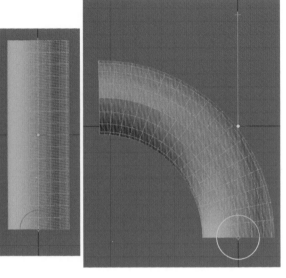

# Removing Mesh Geometry

## *The Delete vs. the Backspace Keys*

> DELETE key: Delete selection (but leave a hole)
>
> BACKSPACE key: Delete selection (but fill in the hole)

Removing geometry is done by selecting the polygon, edge or vertex and hitting either the BACKSPACE key or the DELETE key.

There IS a difference between these keys: DELETE will remove the adjacent polygons if vertex or edge is selected, while BACKSPACE will just remove the vertex or edge; i.e.:

1) Loop select an edge.

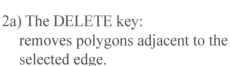

2a) The DELETE key:
   removes polygons adjacent to the selected edge.

- OR -

2b) The BACKSPACE key:
   removes the selected edge. The adjacent polygons get bigger to fill in the mesh.

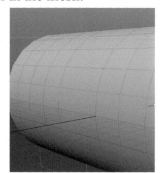

You must change to Wireframe mode (or use the middle mouse button) if you want to select polygons, vertices or edges THROUGH the object onto the other side (note the lasso selection method).

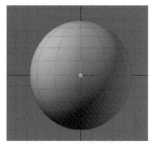
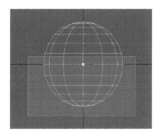
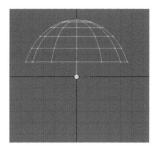
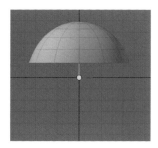

## *Joining Edges and Vertices*

Edge and/or Vertex Join:
   joins the 1st edge/vertex selected to the 2nd edge/vertex selected.

# Adding Mesh Geometry

L key: Loop select

ALT-C: Loop slice

There are several ways to add edges to a mesh/across polygons.

## *Polygon Slice*

1) Select an orthogonal (i.e. front, top, side) view.

2) Select Edge mode.

3) Select Mesh Edit -> Slice.

4) Drag the slice across the polygon face.

5) Hit spacebar to drop the tool. The slice will become a new edge on the mesh.

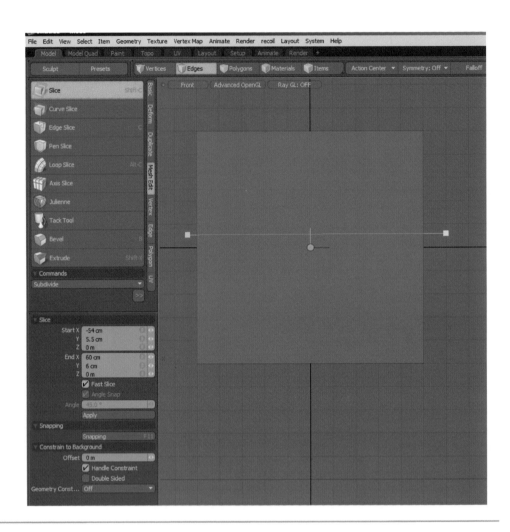

## *Loop Slice*

Loop slicing on a polygon will add edges to create strips. Select one of the edges of these strips and Loop Slice the edge again to create another set of edges at right angles to the first set (to give you squares).

The Loop Slice shortcut is ALT-C, i.e., select a loop of polygons (via the L key), then use ALT-C.

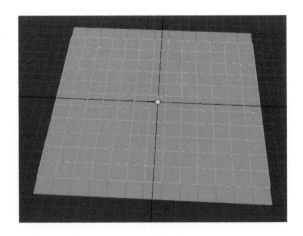

B key: Bevel

Z key: Edge/Polygon extend

P key: Polygon fill

## *Edge Bevel*

The Bevel (B key) works differently on polygons, vertices and edges. It can be used to turn one edge into two edges.

*   The opposite of his is Edge Join (where you join the 1st edge selected into the 2nd edge selected).

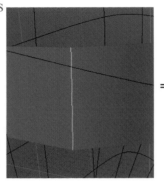 => 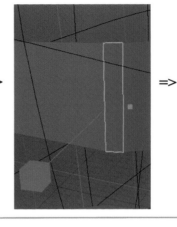 =>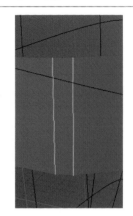

## *Edge Slide*

Use Edge Slide to reposition an Edge

*   Sometimes the edge slide drags surrounding geometry along with it. Sometimes not.

## *Edge Extend*

The Z key will extend an edge (of a polygon).

## *Polygon Fill*

The P key will fill in a polygon, if its surrounding edges (or vertices) are selected.

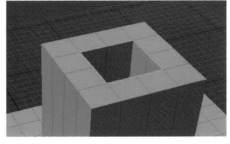 

# Subdividing

SHIFT-D: Show subdivisions popup

P Key: Polygon fill

The D key (for subdividing) is a convenient way to further subdivide an entire mesh, but it distorts/rounds off the shape. Sometimes you want this round off.

 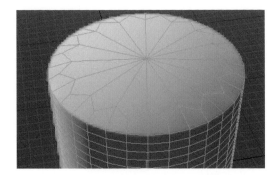

## *SDS (SubDivision Surfaces)*

Use SHIFT-D to get subdivision options (Faceted, Smooth, ...). These will subdivide a mesh **without distorting its shape**.

- The SHIFT-D option won't work if the mesh is Item selected (rather than polygon, vertex or edge selected).

Catmull-Clark Subdivision properties are in the lower right:

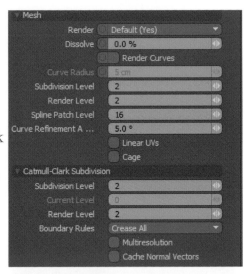

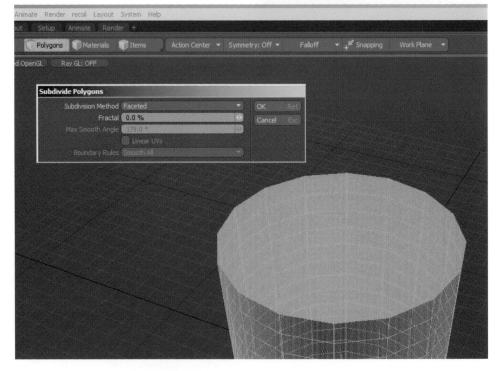

## *SubDivision Options*

SHIFT-D: Bring up subdivision popup menu

TAB, SHIFT TAB: Toggle corner edge rounding

ALT-C: Insert edges into a polygon loop selection

D key: Subdivide a mesh selection

| | |
|---|---|
| Faceted       -- looks like --   Smooth. | No edge rounding.<br>Adds polygons. |
| SDS Subdivide  -- looks like---  Catmull-Clark. | Rounds off edges.<br>No additional polygons. |
| TAB key, SHIFT-TAB key (Pixar subdivision). | Rounds off edges.<br>No additional polygons.<br>•   Hitting TAB again reverts to the original no rounding. |

## *Control Edges*

The TAB and SHIFT-TAB (Pixar subdivisions) will toggle corner rounding subdivisions. "Control edges" control how large the round radius is.

No/minimal control edges:

We will get a larger radius after the TAB key is hit.

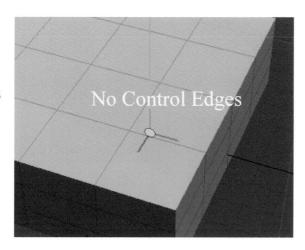

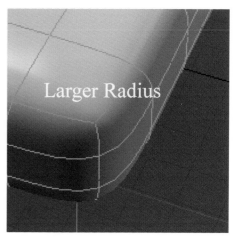

Control edges

Edge slide an edge loop so the edge is near the corner.

You can use Alt-C to insert edges into a polygon loop selection if needed.

These tighten the radius after the TAB key is hit.

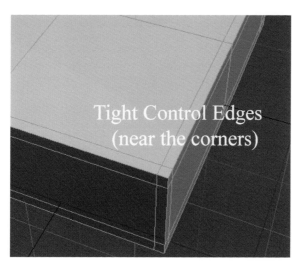

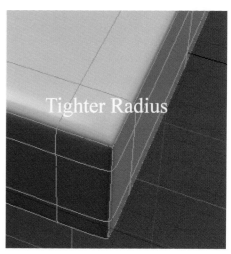

# Curve Extrude, Bridging

1) Select the polygon you want to extrude in perspective view.

2) Select Duplicate -> Curve Extrude.

3) Click on the polygon again.

4) Change to an orthogonal (e.g. front) view

- It's hard to extrude in the perspective view and not get unwanted twists in the geometry.

5) Click-click-click... an extrude path.

- You can adjust the control vertices after each click if needed.  You'll find that it's a bit like adjusting a slinky.

Curve Extrude is often followed by a Polygon Bridge (e.g., for a coffee cup handle).

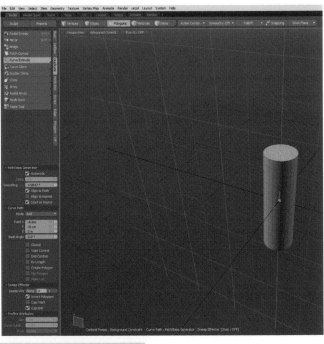
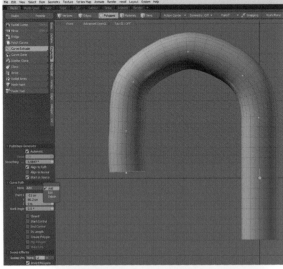

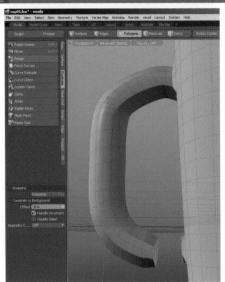

Bridging is also done between edges to create new polygons.

- TRICK!: when bridging a series of edges (i.e. a seam), you want the same number of edges (= the same number of vertices dividing up the edges) on each side of the bridge. This is not always easy and takes some foresight when creating the initial geometry.

- Although used in other places, bridging (along with Z key polygon edge extend, and beveling an edge to create two edges) is important in patch modeling (e.g. when adding polygons to detail a face, see: "Patch Modeling a Face").

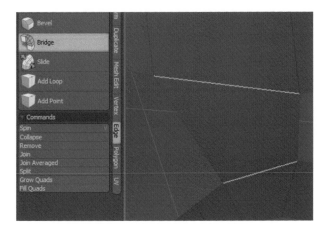

You can split a single edge into two (or more) edges by adding points to it.

- This sometimes helps you to get the same number of edges on each side of a seam that you are bridging.

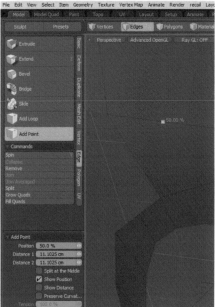

You don't bridge vertices. You join them using Vertex Join. (If not averaging a vertex join) the first vertex selected is moved over to join the second vertex selected.

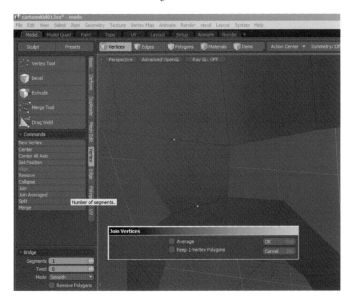

# Pegs And Holes

Cntrl-Backspace: Collapse

## *Round Peg Coming Out Of Square Polygons*

Note: It's easier to do this next section WITHOUT subdivisions turned on (use the Tab key to toggle subdivisions off-on).

The goal is to take 4 polygons in a square and draw an X through them.

* Then one can select the center vertex and bevel it out to create the round (actually octagonal) peg.
* Note that the surrounding geometry at the base of the round peg will all be quads (which is good. We want 4 sided polygons as much as possible).

1) Select 4 polygons of a square.

2) Polygon Triple.

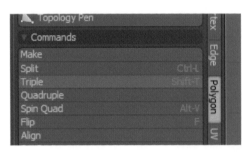

3) Select these two edges.

4) Edge Spin.

* If you've selected the correct edges, this will give you the X through the 4 polygons.

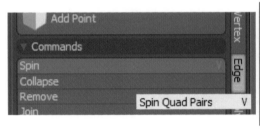

* Selecting 4 polygons (or even a center vertex), then using Cntrl-Backspace (aka "Collapse") will create a variant of this X effect.

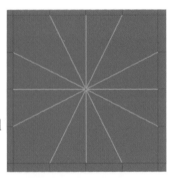

5) Select middle vertex and bevel it out (via the B key).

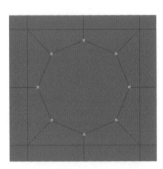

6) Bevel (via the B key) or Extrude out the top polygon to create a peg.

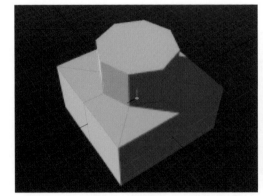

7) You can bevel an additional time at the corners to get control edges to control radii when subdividing.

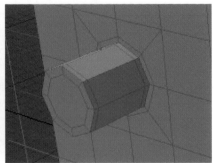

# Round Hole In A Square

Bevel out a vertex as previously described, then:

1) Select both ends.

2) Check the Remove Polygons box of the Bridge:

3) Click on a selected area to make the hole.

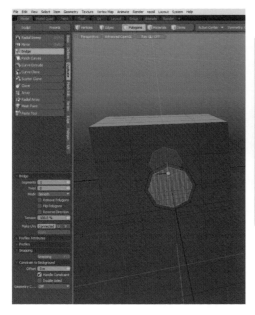

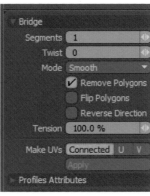

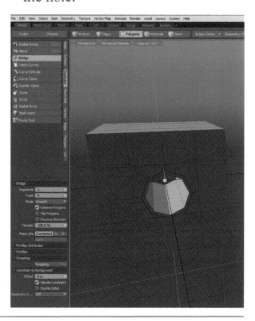

# Making Holes Using Booleans

This isn't as nice as the above Bridging method, because the polygons won't necessarily be a "flow of quads" .

1) Put the drilling object Item layer (a cylinder in this case) **below** the Item layer you want the hole in (so that the drilling / subtracted layer is in the "background").

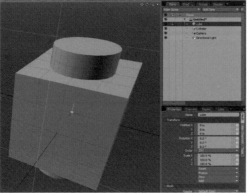

2) Select: Geometry -> Boolean -> Boolean.

3) Choose Subtract and hit OK.

4) Hide (or delete) the background (e.g. cylinder) layer.

- You can hide an Item layer by clicking on the little eyeball in the Item list.

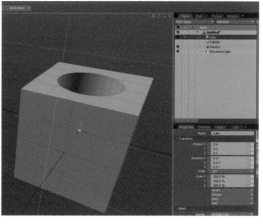

# Fixing Mesh Geometry

## *Automatic Mesh Cleanup*

Geometry ->
Mesh Cleanup.

## *Finding Isolated Vertices*

1) The Lists->Statistics list (in the lower right) shows you which vertices are not connected to any polygons or edges (= connected to 0).

2) Clicking on the + sign to the left lets you select them for deletion.

- In the screenshot below, there are 15 isolated vertices not connected to anything.

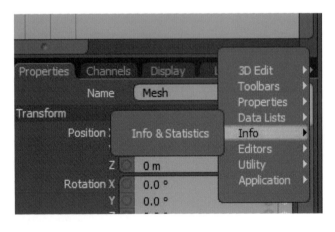

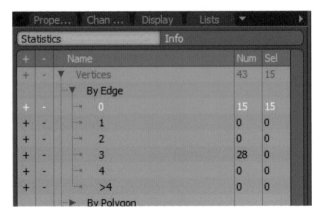

## *Manual Fixes*

More manual ways to fix mesh geometry (especially if polygons and/or edges get overlapped or twisted around each other) are:

- Deleting edges and vertices.
- Edge Join.
- Vertex Join.

# Mesh Centers

I have found working with mesh centers one of the more important and overlooked aspects of modo® books and tutorials. Hopefully this summary will help!

## *Polygon vs Item Selection & Mesh Center Movement*

### *Sometimes Mesh Centers Don't Move With A Mesh*

If you double click on one of the polygons of a mesh to select the entire mesh, then move the mesh, the center of the mesh will stay where it was. An illustration of this (and how the center of rotation is affected) is as follows:

1) Start a new scene. With NONE of the Action Centers selected.
2) Use the O key to set: Show Centers [Selected].
3) Place a cube in the viewport.

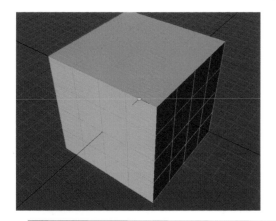

4) In Polygon mode, double click on a polygon to select the mesh.
5) Move the mesh. Note that the center stays.

- If you selected the mesh in Item mode and moved it, the center would have moved along with it.

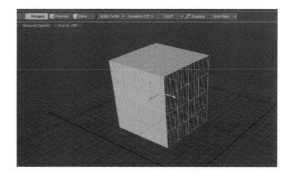

6) After double clicking on a polygon to select the mesh, select the rotation tool.
- Note that **the rotation is around the local mesh selection, even though its center is off to the side.**

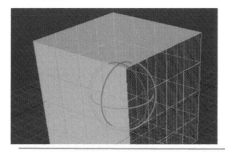

7) Drop the rotation tool (via the spacebar).
8) Deselect the mesh (via left mouse clicking in a blank part of the viewport).
9) Select the mesh in **Item mode.**
10) Select the rotate tool.
- Note that **rotation is now around the center (that is off to the side).**

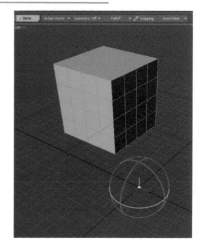

Note: if you have the Action Center set to origin the center will also stay behind when you move the mesh.

# *Moving the Center Of A Mesh*

| O key: Bring up visibility popup menu |
| --- |

**YOU WILL PROBABLY USE THIS A LOT!**

1) To make sure you can see the center of a selected
mesh, use the O key and make sure
   Show Centers [Selected]
is set.

2) Select polygons whose center you want to
become the center of the mesh. Select the
Work Plane dropdown (top right of screen),
then select "Align Work Plane to Selection".

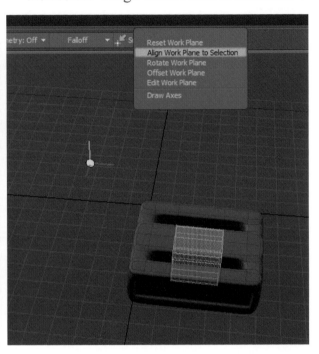

3) Under the Setup tab, (a) select the rectangular
"Centers" button (it will turn yellow), (b) then select
the center (the middle white circle will turn amber).

4) Select the Work Plane dropdown (top right
of screen) and reset the Work Plane.

(c) then (under the Setup vertical tab on left) select:
Set
   To Work Plane Position.
This will snap the center to the new mesh center.

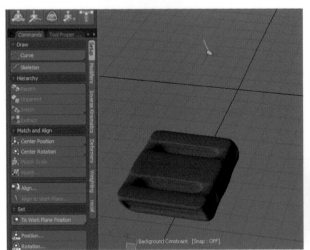

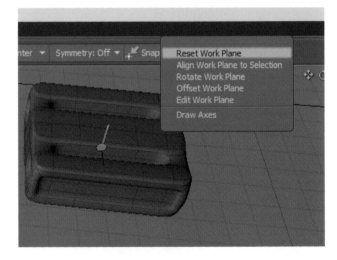

## *A Common Centering Problem*

If you (e.g.) cut and paste some of the polygons from one Item layer into another Item layer, the center of the polygons in the new Item layer stay where it was in the original mesh.

> CNTRL-X: Cut, put in the clipboard
>
> CNTRL-V: Paste from the clipboard
>
> N key: Create new mesh layer in Item list

e.g.: Try cutting a pedal from the tricycle mesh (select the pedal's polygons by double clicking on one of them, then CNTRL-X to cut) that comes with modo® (under the Layout tab, in the Miscellaneous category) and pasting the pedal onto another Item Layer (use the N key to make a new Item layer, then CNTRL-V to paste).

HINT: It also helps to rotate the mesh so that it is orthogonally aligned. This is easier to do under the Model Quad view. Do this BEFORE you adjust the mesh center. That way, both the center AND the mesh are orthogonally oriented, making for further alignment with other (hopefully also orthogonally oriented) parts/meshes.

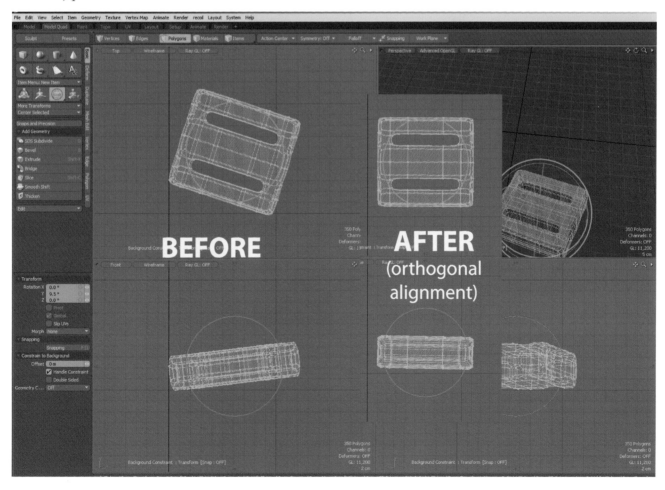

# Lining One Mesh Up With Another

Meshes line up on their centers (unless the Compensation button is selected).

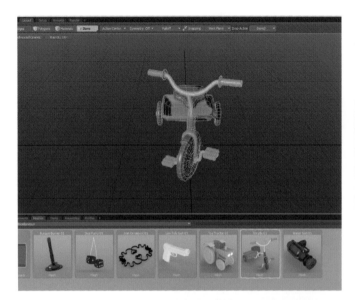
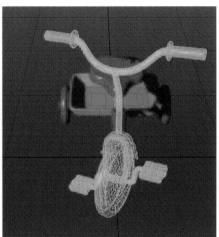

As pointed out in the previous section, it helps to rotate the polygon meshes so that they are orthogonally aligned.

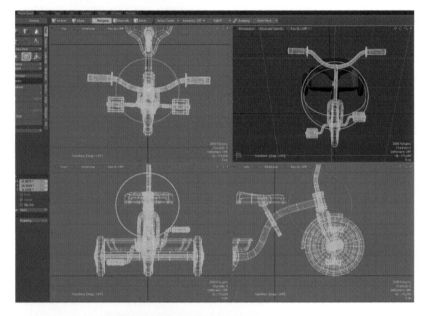

Suppose we want to align the right pedal mesh (on its own layer) to the right pedal axle mesh (on another Item layer).

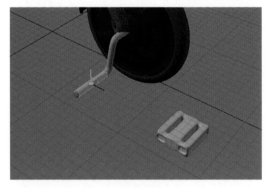

Other than manually moving and rotating the pedal onto the axle, there are two more automatic and accurate ways to do this:

**Method 1:** Use a Drop Action.

1) Set the drop action to (e.g.) Match.

2) Select the item from the layer under the Items list (the right pedal is selected in this example).

Then:

3) Drag it from the Item List right onto the right pedal axle in the viewport.

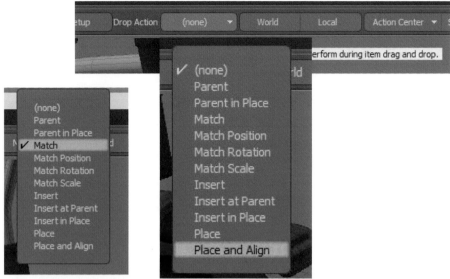

**Method 2:** Use Match and Align (under the vertical Setup tab on the left) .

1) First: Select the mesh you will be aligning (in this case the pedal).

2) Second: Hold down the shift key and select the mesh you will be aligning it to (in this case, the pedal axle).

The select:

  Match and Align
    Item Position

and/or

    Item Rotation.

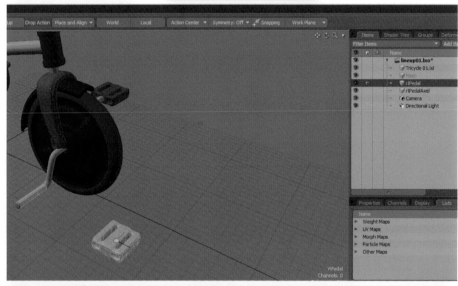

Under either of the above methods, the pedal center should automatically snap into alignment with the pedal axle center.

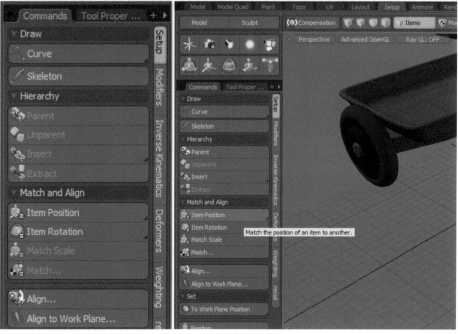

# Importing Reference Images

1) Under the Items tab (in upper right) select: Add Item -> Backdrop Item.

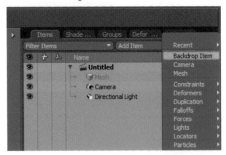

2) The backdrop item appears. We still have to put a picture on it.

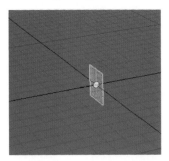

3) Click on the Image square under properties in the lower right:

4) Add Clip > (load image).

5) Set the Projection Type (e.g. front, right side,...) under properties in the lower right:

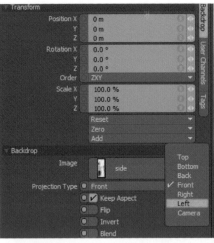

6) Reduce the Transparency down to about 70%

- This assumes the image is a .png or 32 bit jpg (which has an alpha channel and can therefore be made transparent).

7) Finally, check:

System -> Preferences -> OpenGL -> Flatness of Perspective.

is set to around 60%. This setting imitates a 35mm camera and makes the reference images more accurate at oblique angles.

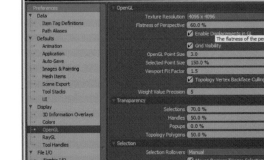

# Organic (e.g. Character) Modeling

There are lots of ways to do this. Here's one way (that I would not have guessed) from one of the Luxology tutorials, in which the basic organic shape is created. Its surface can then act as a background constraint for the further (polygon-by-polygon) detailed patch modeling:

Assuming you have a background image centered at the origin:
1) Turn symmetry on in the X.
2) Select the Solid Sketch tool.

3) Right mouse click on the Y axis parting line (at X=0) to put down the first glob of mesh. Use the handles to shape the clay-like mesh (this takes a little practice).

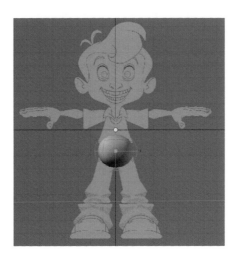

4) Change to SubDiv Mode [Level 2] (in the lower left side panel).

5) Click on a mesh node (where you want to branch from), then click where you want to go to (towards the neck in this case).

6) Shape, click on a node, extend (often to a character joint, such as a knee or elbow), repeat.

• You might have to switch from the front to a side view to do parts that stick out forward (like the feet).

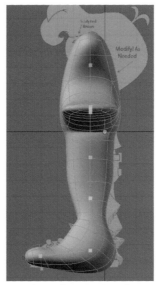

*\* Cartoon Kid drawing courtesy Darren Hunt of Push Pen Studios (pushpenstudios.carbonmade.com).*

7) To more finely define the mesh, use Mesh Sculpting to shrink, expand or move part of the mesh.

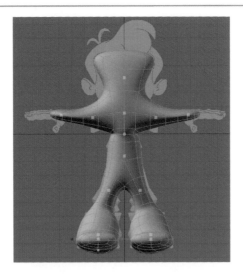

> D key: Subdivide
>
> SHIFT key: For sculpting, will do the opposite

## *Mesh Sculpting*

8) After selecting a tool, right mouse click to adjust the size of your brush.

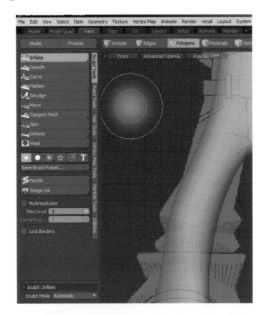

Holding down the SHIFT key will do the opposite of what's selected in the Mesh Sculpting menu.

- e.g. holding down the SHIFT key for inflate will deflate.

9) Slowly drag the brush along the mesh to bulk out or shrink it in (paint brush sized) areas.

- Press D to add another level of subdividing as needed.

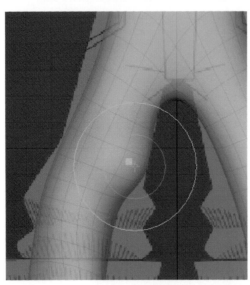

(Mesh) move also comes in handy when sculpting the mesh.

Note: Further instructions for patch modeling the character's face are given under "Background Constraints".

# MATERIALS

1) Make an Item or Polygon selection. Then press the M key.

2) Name the material in the popup box that appears.

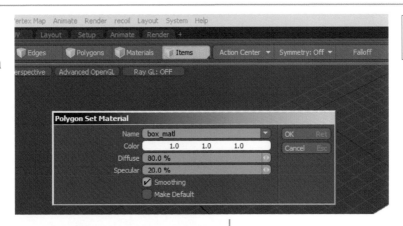

M key: Assign material to selection

3) Go to the Shader tab in the upper right of the screen.

4) Optional: Select the Material. The Material properties can be adjusted in the lower right of the screen.

e.g.: clicking on the Diffuse Color lets you change the color.

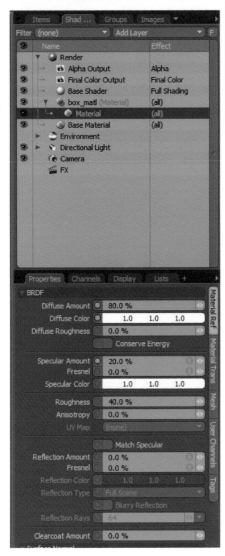

## Dropping In A Layout Material

5) Go to the Layout tab in the upper part of the screen. Select a material from the lower section of the Layout screen.

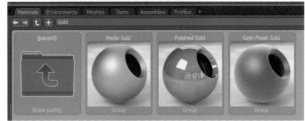

6) Drag the material over to the Shader Tree, and drop it directly under the (e.g.) box_matl. This will insert it and override the Material below it.

* The upper items the Shader Tree override the lower items.

# USING IMAGE MAPS

Image maps wrap around a mesh and can give it a LOT of detail without increasing the polygon count.

## Creating A UV Map

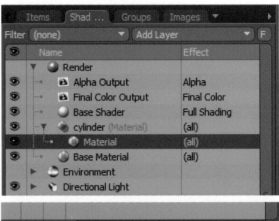

1) Select the item. Press M to create a material for it, as described in the previous section.

2) Select the material in the Shader Tree (cylinder in this case).

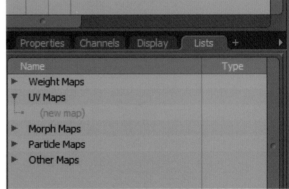

3) Select "(new map)" under Lists, UV Maps in the lower right.

4) OPTIONAL: Sometimes you want to select the edges which will act as the "seam" for the UV map.

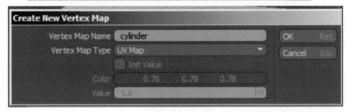

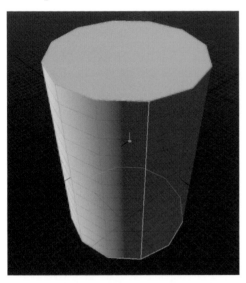

5) Set the iterations at around 1000.

6) Click on the Unwrap Tool, then click in the UV viewport. The UV map should appear.

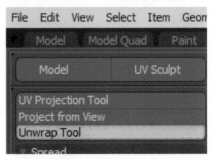

7) Select UV Relax, make sure the mode is set to Unwrap, and click in the viewport. This relaxes the mesh a little.

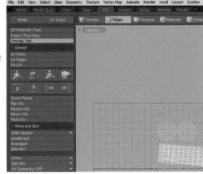

Advanced Note: You can move and scale the pieces of the UV map. Scaling the UV map can affect how fine a (e.g.) bump map appears.

Note how selecting a polygon on the UV map will also select the corresponding polygon on the mesh.

8) To save the map as an image:

Go to the Paint tab, Utilities and click Add ... Texture.

- Displacement Textures will be good for bump, normal and displacement maps.

- Color Textures are for painting on the image with color.

Even with a high end graphics computer, the higher the map resolution, the more delay there will be between brush strokes as you paint on the map.

9) OPTIONAL: To apply an image to the map (instead of 8):

Go to the Shader Tree->Add Layer->Image Map->(load image).

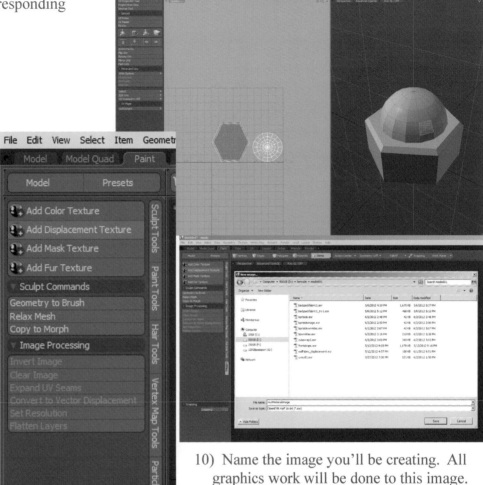

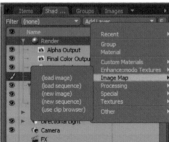

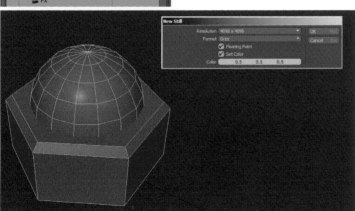

10) Name the image you'll be creating. All graphics work will be done to this image.

(i.e., you will be doing image based sculpting instead of geometry based sculpting).

The image map should automatically appear in the Shader Tree.

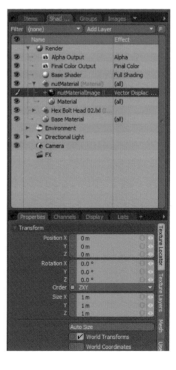

# Image Based Sculpting

F8: Render preview

SHIFT: Opposite painting/sculpting effect

11) Right click to change the Vector Displacement (map) to a Displacement (map) (because this is a grey scale map).

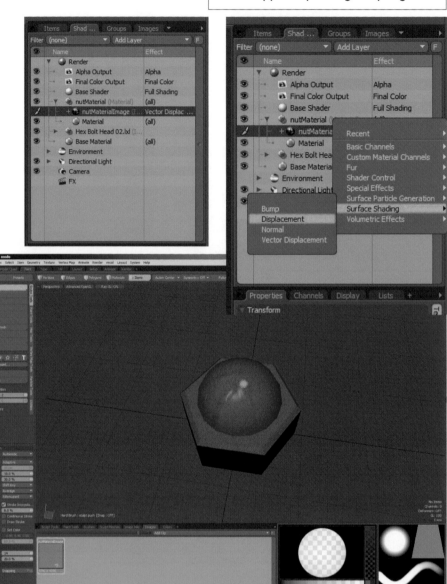

12) Sculpt using the Paint tab. Choose an effect and start painting. Right click to change the size of the paint brush.

- Note the white on the UV map image in the lower left. White means the geometry is coming towards you, black means recessed or away from you.

Sometimes you have to use F8 (render preview) to see the effect of painting.

Left mouse button on the little arrow in the lower right of each sculpting option will bring up more painting options. Inflate is the opposite of push. The SHIFT key will give you opposite option effects as well.

# Surface Shading Maps

To put this (kenfreedsoftware.png):

# Ken Freed Software

image on a mesh as a surface shader:

Using the same UV Image, Blend Mode [Subtract] (under properties in the lower right):

Bump Map

Displacement Map

Normal Map

Vector Displacement Map

1) Select all the polygons of the mesh (by double clicking on one of the mesh's polygons). Hit the M key to assign a material (which we are naming "cylinder" in this case).

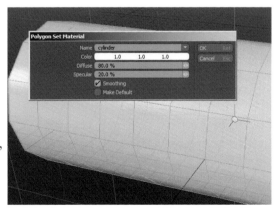

2) Select Add Layer in the Shader Tree, then Image Map, (load image).

3) Make sure Ray GL is ON - so you can see the map.

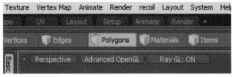

4) Adjusting the Properties, Texture Locator (in the lower right): **the hardest thing is to get the image located where you want it.** Try changing:

        Projection Type: [Planar].

        Projection Axis: try each of X, Y, Z.

        Horizontal/Vertical Repeat: Reset (for only one repeat).

        Transform: Play with all the options. Try different map types until something shows up.

5) After you have the image located, right click on the image type and click Bump, Normal or Displacement Map.

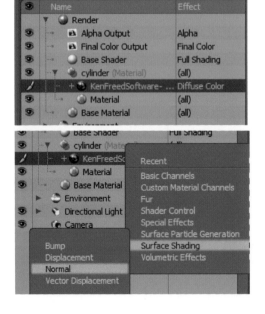

6) Then select a Blend Mode under properties, Texture Layers.

- Since black is recessed and white is towards you, some of these bland modes might make the image disappear.

Shown: a Bump Map with a Blend Mode of Subtract, laid over a glossy plastic surface.

# *Procedural Surface Shading Maps*

1) Take a sphere, select all its polygons (by double clicking on one of its polygons), and press M to assign a material (named "sphere" in this example).

2) Under the Shader tab (upper right), right click on Diffuse Color and change it to Bump map.

3) Right click again to set the "Procedural Texture" of the bump map to Dots.

4) Tricky Part: As with other maps, play with the Texture Locator to get the bumps sized and positioned, then tweak the Texture Layers properties for the desired effect.

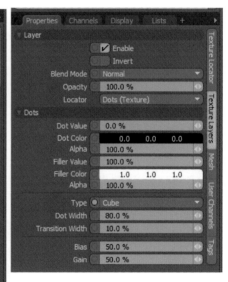

5) Here is the final (golf ball-like) sphere after locating in a camera view and pressing F9 to render:

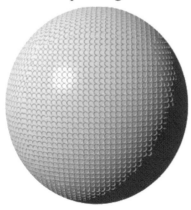
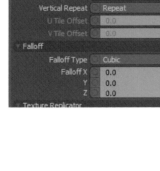

# RENDERING

Even though rendering is probably intended to be done from the Camera view, I find using F10 to render the current (usually Modeling tab) view quicker when developing a scene.

F8: Render preview

F9: Render camera view

F10: Render current view

The Camera view can be obtained by either choosing the Render tab (at the top of the screen), or changing to Camera view under the Modeling tab:

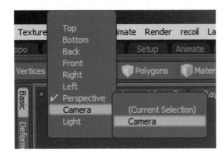

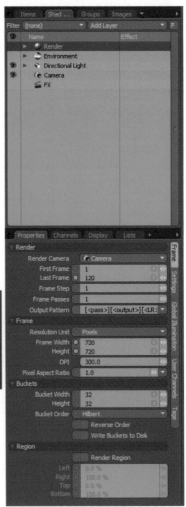

## *The size of the render is set under the Shader Tree:*

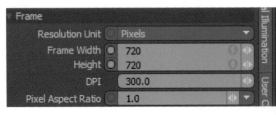

Use
72 DPI for web images, and
300 DPI for images that will be printed.

# LIGHTING

## Adding Lights

O key: Bring up visibility popup

Lights are added as shown to the right:

- Use either Area Lights or Portal Lights to shine light in through window openings.

Lights are moved, rotated (etc.) via their properties and NOT via the move, rotate (etc.) manipulators.

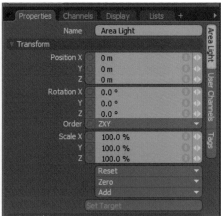

To view the lights in a scene, press the "O" key and check the "Show Lights" option.

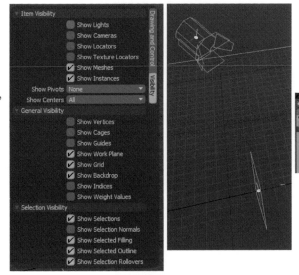

There are also a few lights under the Layout tab->Items.

Although used for "volumetric" effects, the "Sprite" can also have a plasma glow ball lighting effect.

The Spite is moved via the standard (move, rotate etc) manipulators.

# Background Lighting

With no background, the modo® render space is "black space" in a .png image output (i.e., it will be transparent). For other image types (e.g. jpg) the background is a default gray gradient. If you want something else, you need some sort of backdrop for the light to bounce off of. One of the backdrops included with modo® is a "Shadow Catcher":

Luxology asset sharing at http://community.thefoundry.co.uk/asset/ has a Sweep background. You can also make your own by bending a plane (using either bend, or a linear falloff with a rotation).

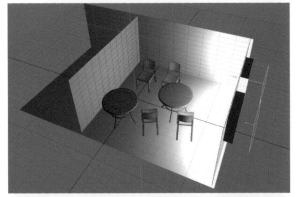

This example shows area lights shining through the windows, with a little bit of global illumination.

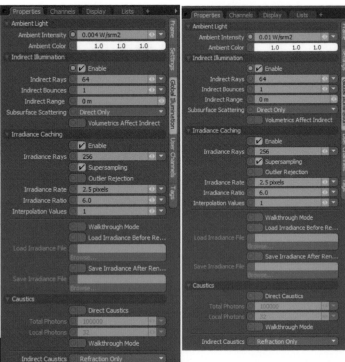

Area lights bounced off a backdrop with some Global Illumination:

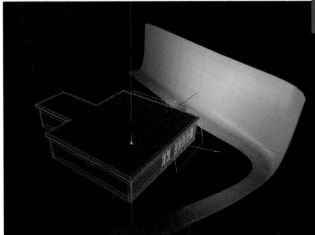

*Exterior*

*Interior*

# Interior Lighting

Enable Global Illumination for:
- Interior renders.
- Renders where more even surrounding light is needed.

You usually have to Enable and use at least some Global Illumination to get decent interior fill-in lighting.

When global illumination is enabled, the render (F9) will develop differently (as dots or pixels, rather than squares or buckets).

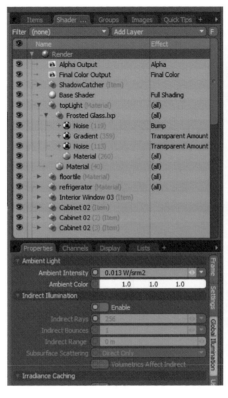

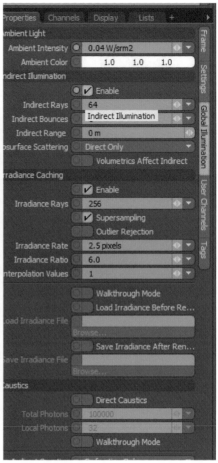

---

# Base Shader (Global)

Shaders provide additional exterior lighting effects.

- Move the (global) Base Shader up in the hierarchy to be over the items to which it applies:

If you use a Local Shader, make sure you drag the mesh it applies to above the global Base Shader under the Render tab.

# Local Shader

- To provide more specific lighting, you can add a local shader TO A MESH by clicking on Add Layer:

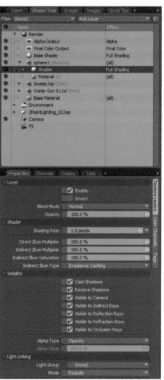

The Shading Rate is the first thing you'll change to get rid of noise/graininess.

# Exterior Renders, Sun Effects

There's a "Sun" effect under the properties for directional lights:

- Modo®'s default is a single directional light.

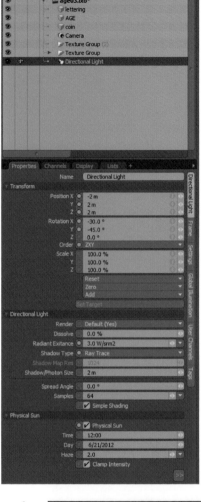

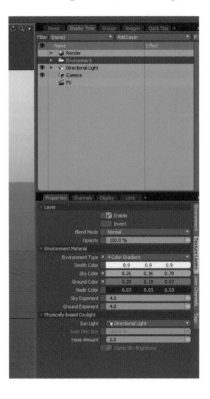

The is also a "Sun" effect under the Shader Tree

Environment ->Environment Material.

Set the Environment Type to Physically Based Light. Then select the Directional Light and click the Physically Based Sun checkbox (as before):

If you get a lot of bright spots or streaks, dial down the "Affect Specular" value:

# Cleaning Up Noisy Renders

Interior renders typically have a higher number of reflective surfaces than exterior renders (and therefore tend to have more "blotchy" noise problems). Noise (or grainy areas) are best addressed by:

(1) Using more light rays in the render or
(2) By decreasing the rays skipped over in the filtering.
(3) By adding more ray trace bounces to pick up more indirect lighting.

- Sometimes the ray exiting the light source counts as the first bounce.

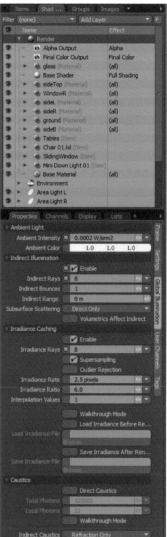

If the render looks grainy try increasing:

- Indirect Rays.
- Irradiance Rays.

Irradiance Caching is filtering/short cutting for irradiance ray calculations. These are complex. The 2 parameters to try adjusting are:

- Irradiance Rate.
- Irradiance Ratio.

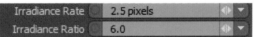

In general: Irradiate Rate x Irradiance Ratio = pixels skipped over during ray bounce calculations (in the less detailed areas).

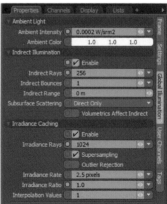

Once again, if you have graininess or blotchy artifacts (which usually comes with more rays bouncing off of more meshes), firing more rays is the 1st approach to cleaning it up. The 2nd approach is increasing the global anti-aliasing or dropping the Ray Threshold (causes less rays to be ignored).

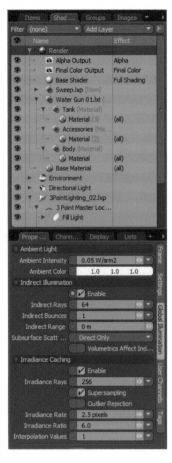
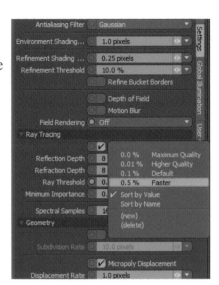

Some of these numeric parameters give you lower or higher quality renders at the cost of render time. They mostly correct for graininess and blotchy artifacts.

They're the ones to change when trying to improve a render.

Worse Settings (jagged edges):

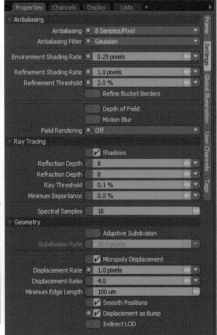

Better Settings:

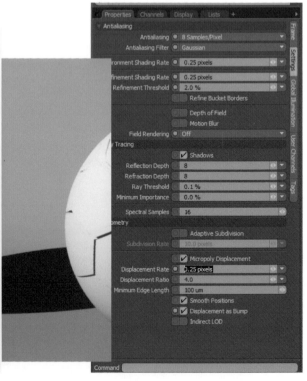

# RIGGING/CONSTRAINTS

Rigging is a type of constraint. Constraints are the control of one item from the manipulation (movement, rotation, etc.) of another. Rigging/constraints are set up under the "Setup" tab (which would be more appropriately named the "Rigging" tab). Rigging is always done prior to animation.

- The "Animation" tab has some of the same functions as the "Setup" tab.

1) FIRST select the item that will be constrained
2) THEN select the item that the first one will be constrained to.
2b) Optionally: Select the Compensation button if you want the (first) constrained item to stay where it is (and not snap/rotate etc. to the position of the second item).

- The Compensate button automatically calculates and fills in the Constraint (position, etc.) Offsets.

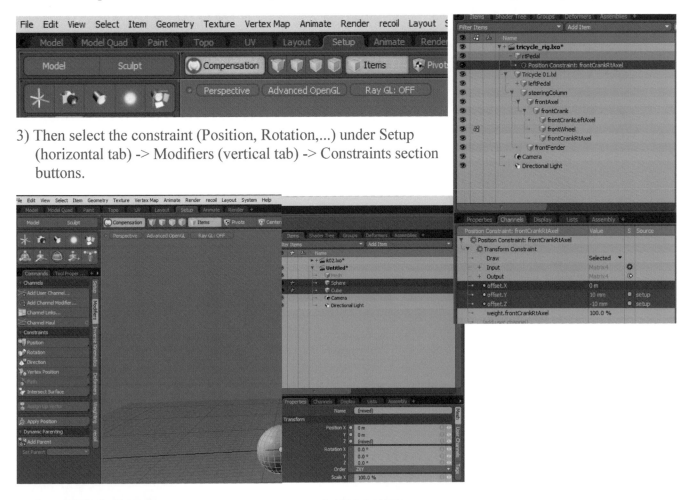

3) Then select the constraint (Position, Rotation,...) under Setup (horizontal tab) -> Modifiers (vertical tab) -> Constraints section buttons.

 Right clicking brings up more constraint options:

Dragging the constraint from the Item list into the channel area (mid bottom of the screenshot below) displays its representation as a channel.

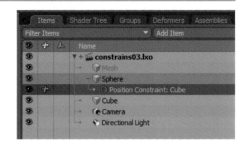

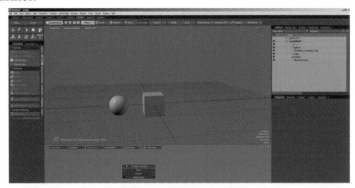

Middle mouse button clicking on the circles outlined in yellow will bring up their connections.

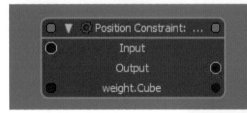

**CONFUSION SOURCE:** Right mouse button clicking in the channel area and choosing "clear" will ONLY clear the **display** of the channel/constraint. It will NOT clear the constraint itself, i.e. you can just drag the constraint down again to see its representation in channel form.

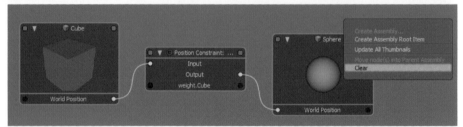

Note: The channels shown in the lower part of the screen were introduced in modo® 501, and are a cleaner way to show constraint relationships. The internal constraint data/effect are the same whether you use the channel display to see constraints, or use the Setup (horizontal tab) -> Modifiers (vertical tab) -> Constraints section buttons.

# To Limit A Constraint's Axis

1) Select the constraint, then the "Add Output Modifiers" button.

2) In this example, only the Y axis movement is constrained (meaning the sphere will only follow the cube's movement along the Y axis).

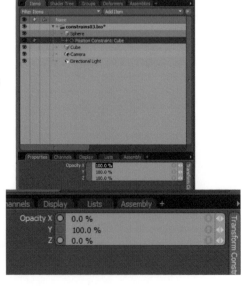

# Rotational Constraints

This is one of the most frequently used constraints.

1) Using the rotate transform, determine which axis your mesh rotates around.

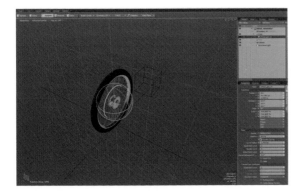

Even though it was by dragging the yellow (Y) axis we rotated the wheel, the axis (or axle) of rotation was around the X.

2) Get the channel for the wheel's x rotation.

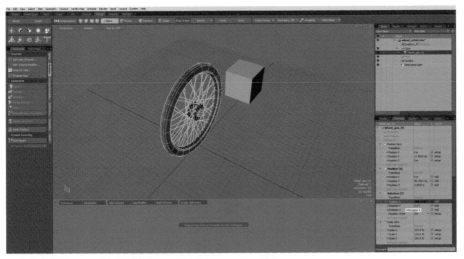

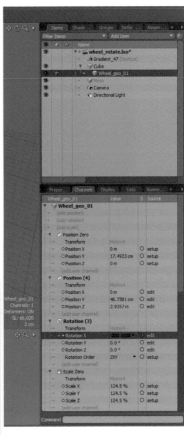

3) Get the World Position for the parent object.

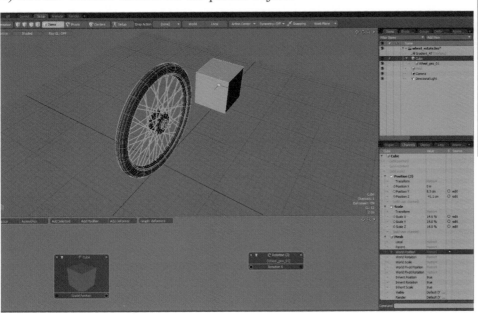

4) Hook up the channel network as follows (inserting the appropriate Revolve and Math:Multiply modifiers in between).

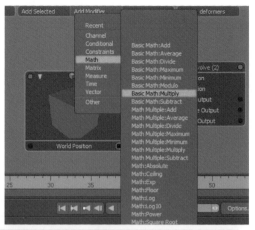

Below is an example of how to get the wheel to rotate when a cube moves.

HINT: If the wheel will only rotate when the cube is moved perpendicular to it, you might have to disconnect the network and rotate the cube by 90 degrees to get this to work out correctly.

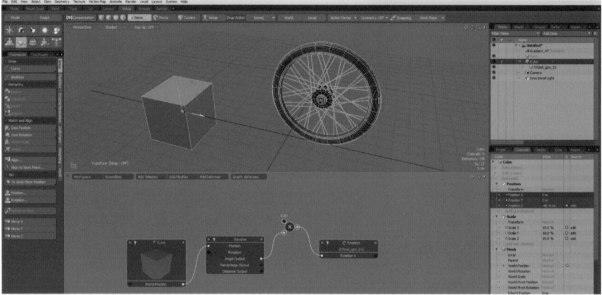

Here's a more extensive scene involving the rotation of 4 wheels when the car body moves.

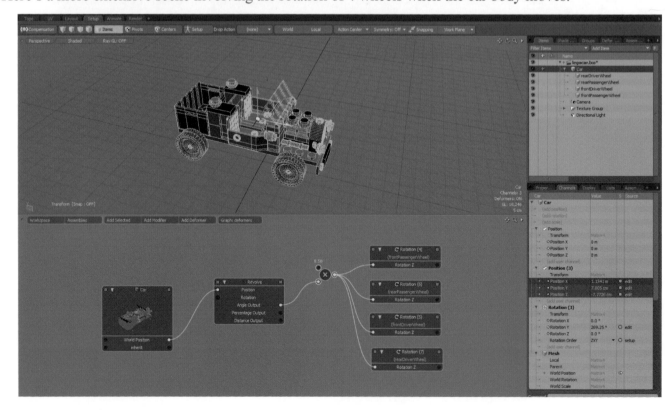

The Revolve modifier has a channel (i.e., data field) for the radius
- This will make the wheel rotate at the right speed when the parent (a tricycle in this case) is moving.

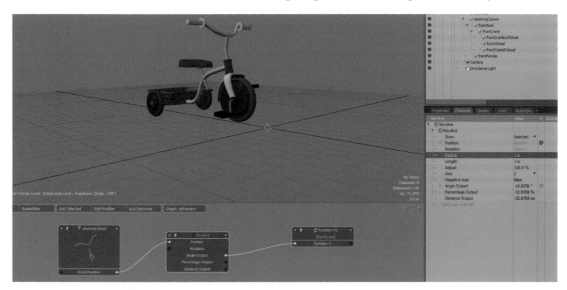

To measure the radius:
1) Go to a left, right, etc. orthogonal view (as appropriate).
2) View -> Dimensions Tool.

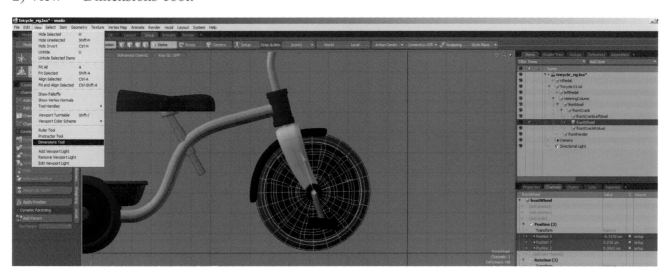

3) Select what you want to measure (the polygons around the edge of the tire in this case).

4) Then enter it as the radius for the Revolve modifier.

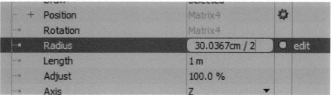

# Creating An IK (Inverse Kinematics) Rig

FK (Forward Kinematics) is a dog wagging its tail.  IK (Inverse Kinematics) is the tail wagging the dog.

IK (Inverse Kinematics) is used to constrain THREE items relative to each other; e.g.:

- a Thigh, Knee, Shin.
- a Upper Arm, Elbow, Forearm.

IMPORTANT: Put exactly THREE items into an IK rig (this is called planar IK, because the 3 item centers form a plane).  You cannot chain more than 3 items (which would be called multilink IK) in modo®.

- In this example we will use a sphere and two cylinders to represent a knee, thigh and shin.

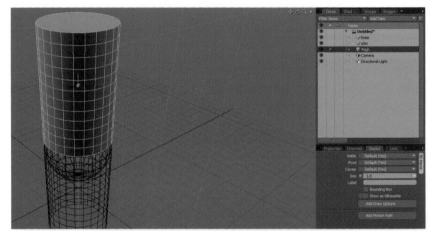

1) In order for IK to take effect, the rig MUST have a bend (a very slight bend will do).

- If the thigh, knee and shin are in a straight line, IK will not know which direction to bend its knee.

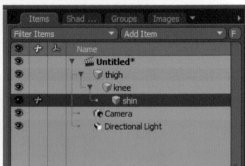

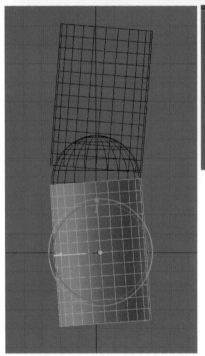

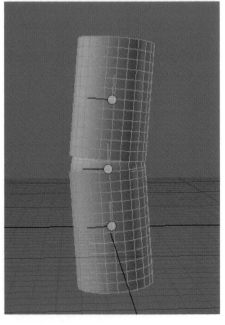

2) The knee's center is OK - but the shin's center (or the point at which it swivels) must be down by the ankle.  Likewise the thigh's center must be moved to be up at the hip.

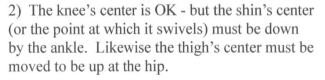

2b) Move the shin (bottom cylinder) and thigh (top cylinder) centers to their rotation points.

**Before:**

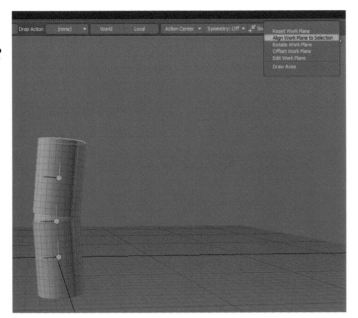

**After:**

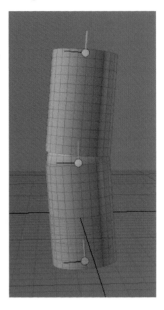

3) Put the three items into a (forward kinematics) hierarchy in the Item list (just drag and drop), with the thigh as the parent, then knee, then shin.

4) Select the item list hierarchy from the top down; i.e. FIRST the thigh, then (holding down the shift key) the Shin. You MUST select the hierarchy from the top down.

5) Then select the Apply IK button.

6) Press "OK" to ignore the warning message that pops up (it has to do with adjusting the IK chain to be planar). The IK constrains will then form.

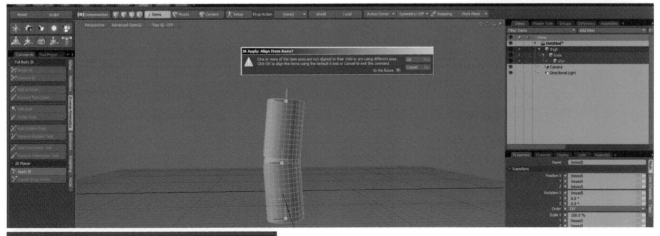

Note that you move the IK chain by the "root" at the top (which is forward kinematics) or by the "goal" at the bottom (which is inverse kinematics).

Selecting and moving the "goal" (an appropriate rename for this would be "ankle").

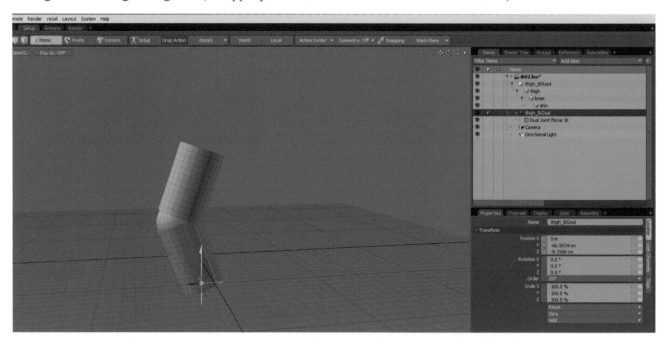

Selecting and moving the "root" (an appropriate rename for this would be "hip_joint").

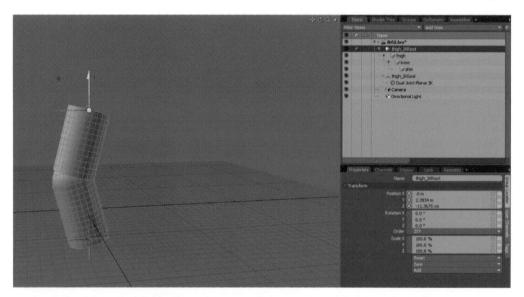

To swivel the knee (which takes the rest of the chain with it), select the "Dual Joint Planar IK" and adjust the Orient.

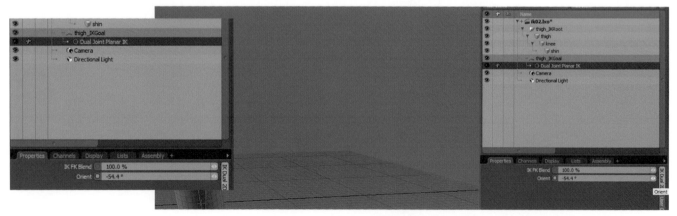

# Background Constraints

Use Background Constraint for (e.g.):

- A cloth draped over a table.
- A geometry "flow" prior to using subdivisions (See: "Joining Two Meshes").

In this example, we will lower a plane onto a sphere and watch it deform around the surface of a sphere.

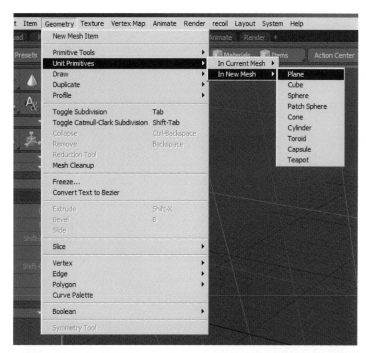

1) Get a plane, and subdivide it using the D key (or polygon select and loop slice, then edge select and further loop slice to create squares) until your polygons are small enough to give you enough resolution to drape the plane over the sphere.

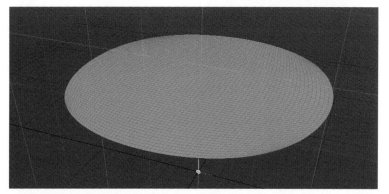

2) Add a sphere to the scene and make sure its layer in the Item List is BELOW that of the plane (i.e. we want it to be below, so it will be used as the "background").

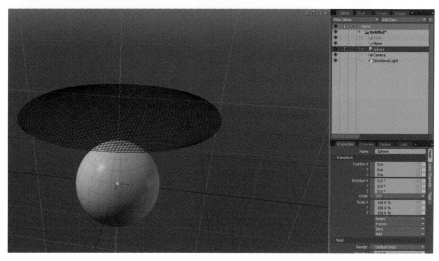

3) Select the Snapping button, then press F11 to bring up the snapping options. Fill the screens out as below. Note that we are showing vector and point (geometry mode) snapping examples.

F11: Snapping options popup

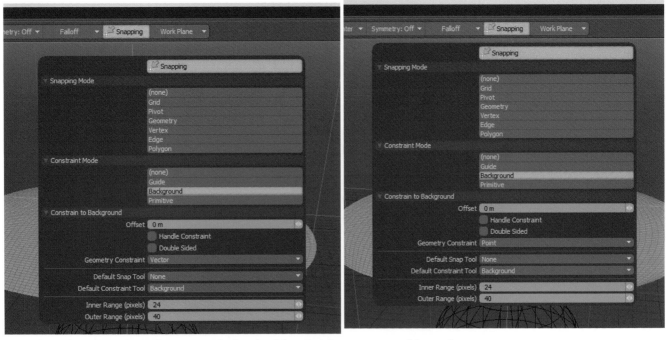

4) Select the plane in polygon mode by double clicking on one of its polygons.

• IMPORTANT - this background constraint will not work if the plane is selected in Item mode.

5) Using the move manipulator, lower the plane onto the sphere.

• In point geometry mode the plane will adhere to the surface, where if can be shifted around.

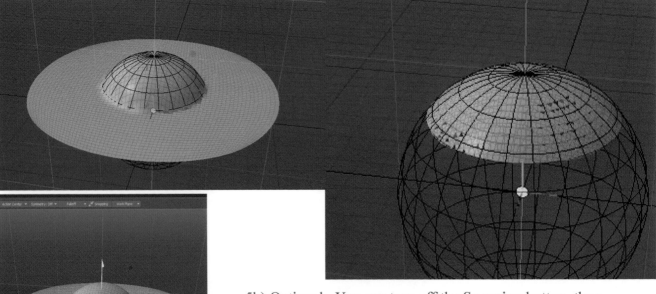

5b) Optional: You can turn off the Snapping button, then lift the plane off of the sphere (using the move tool) to see the impression.

# *Joining Two Meshes*
## Creating Flowing Geometry for Subdividing

This comes up in hard surface modeling.

TAB, SHIFT TAB: Toggle corner rounding

B key: Bevel

R key: Scaling

We want to set up the polygons at the base on the left so that hitting the Tab key (for subdivisions) or Shift Tab (for Pixar subdivisions) will give us a nice rounded transition between the two shapes.

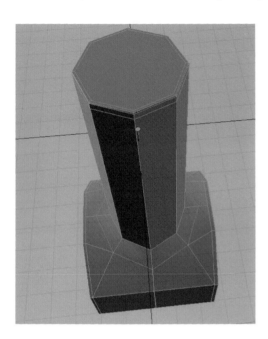

---> TAB key -->

for subdivisions, OR

--> Shift TAB -->

for Pixar subdivisions.

<-- (re) TAB <--
to revert back to the original.

1) Create the handle and head cylinders. Using edge slide and bevel, create the control surfaces (= edges toward the edge of the item to control the subdivision curve radii).

2) Bevel (or Scale) out the end polygon of the handle and background constrain it to the head (as described in the "Background Constraints" section).

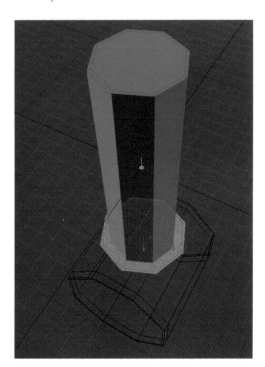

3) Turn off the Snapping used to create the background constraint (or use the escape key).

P key: Polygon fill

Cut the head item from its mesh and paste it into the handle's mesh so we can bridge between the two items (joining them so that they are one mesh).

4) Delete the 3 polygons on the head (as shown below) so we can replace them with bridged polygons.

- Tricky part: You want to try to have the same number of edges facing each other, so that when you use Edge Bridge, you'll get quads (4 sided polygons).

5) Add points as needed so that you have the same number of edges to join. As shown below:

a) Select the edge.
b) Select Add Point as shown.
c) Re-click on the edge.
d) Adjust the Position to (usually) 50%.

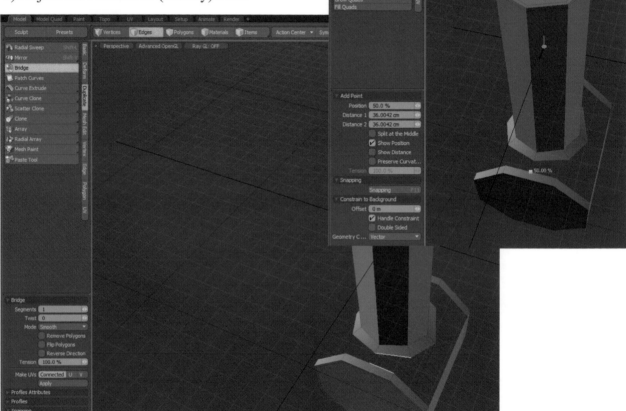

6) Use edge bridging to bridge the handle mesh to the head mesh.

a) Select 2 opposite edges.
b) Select bridging as shown on left.
c) Click in between the two edges. A polygon should appear (as shown).

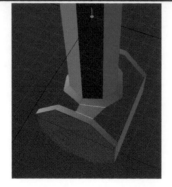

7) When appropriate, use the P key to fill in a polygon after all its surrounding edges are selected.

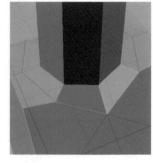

# *Patch Modeling A Face*

Z key: Polygon edge extend

T key: Element move

B key: Bevel

BACKSPACE: Delete selected elements

1) Model the general shape of the head, and set this as the background layer (i.e., put it below the face Item layer that you'll do the patch modeling in). Make this head shape semi transparent so that you can see the reference image through it.

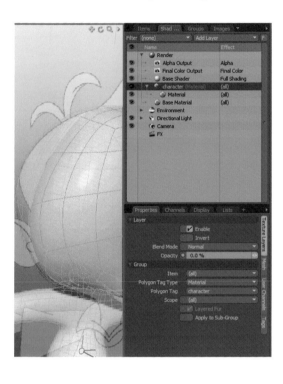 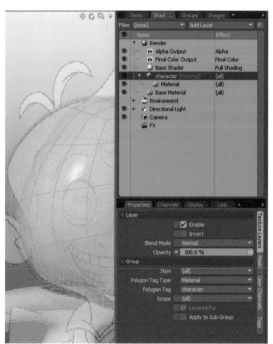

2) Set the background constraint to vector.

3) Use the pen tool and check Make Quads to create strips of polygons representing face muscles.

- You can select the vertices and nudge them along the reference image boundaries as you use the pen tool to create the muscle quads.

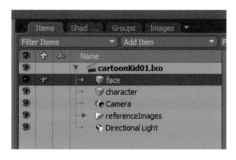

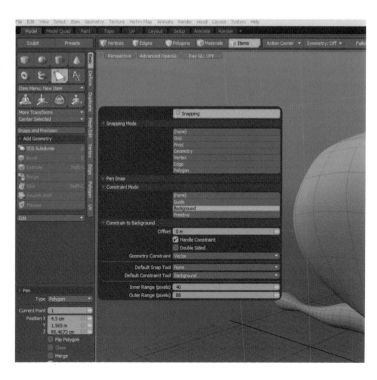

Below are the basic muscles of the face (which will then be mirrored using symmetry to form the other side).

- **Tricky part!**: You want to try to have the same number of edges facing each other, so that when you use Edge Bridge, you'll get quads (4 sided polygons).

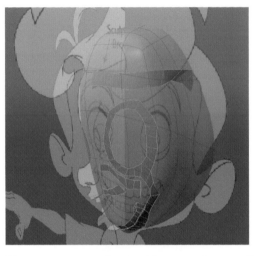

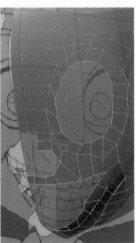

Here are some shortcut keys and operations for patch modeling/quad manipulation:

  Z key : polygon.
  T key: element move.
  Use Edge Bevel: to throw an additional edge in.
  Use Edge Slide: to position the edge.

Use "Edge Join" to combine 2 close edges into one.  Vertex Join is similar.
Use the BACKSPACE key to delete a vertex, edge or polygon.

# APPENDIX

## Taxonomy of 3D Computer Graphics Terms

Those with formal training or lots of experience in computer graphics take the knowledge in this section for granted. For the uninitiated however, it's often hard to find or figure out this overview.

Knowing how 3D graphics software functionality breaks down will help you understand how modo®'s functionality breaks down. Not all 3D graphics software performs all of the functionality which follows (but modo® does).

Please note that the popular Adobe software packages such as Photoshop® and Illustrator® are 2D (not 3D) packages. This means that you cannot take artwork and rotate it to view it from another angle.

| Modeling | How you create an item made up of polygons. | | Other modeling-only software includes: Silo® (~$120). |
|---|---|---|---|
| | Hard Surface & Organic Modeling | Hard surface modeling is for mechanical objects (metal, plastic). | Organic modeling is for humans, animals, cloth, hair. |
| | Box Modeling | Box modeling deforms a starting mesh through extrusion, beveling, moving, etc. . | There are LOTS of ways to deform a (clay-like) mesh of polygons. You have to think through how to deform it to get as many quad polygons as you can. This isn't always self evident at the start and often takes multiple tries. |
| | Point/Patch Modeling | Builds up the mesh, polygon-by-polygon. | This gives you more control over the details, but the overall effect can be out of proportion. Placing polygons upon a background constraint surface helps a LOT. |
| | Subdivisions | Subdivisions round off squared edges of a mesh BUT they do not really affect the underlying base mesh geometry. Edge weighting and/or control edges re-square off (or shrink the radius on) selected rounded edges of the mesh. | If you export a subdivided model to another 3D graphics software package it must support the same subdivision algorithm. Catmull-Clark is somewhat of a standard, while SDS is modo®'s own algorithm. <br>• Edge weighting algorithms are notoriously NOT standard between software packages, so try to use control edges instead. |
| | Retopology | Retopology is for taking the polygons in a mesh and (as much as possible) making them 4 sided (aka "quads"). This helps all 3D graphics software to better process the mesh. | |

| | | Particle Effects | Particle effects are smoke, dust storms, rain etc.<br><br>Bubble gum balls sitting inside a bubble gum machine are also a type of (static) particle effect. | Volumetric lighting effects are for dust particle and fog generation. |
|---|---|---|---|---|
| Texturing | | Texturing is wrapping a mesh/model/object in a "map". This VERY effectively takes the place of having to have more polygon detail in the model. | Some types of maps are: UV Maps, Bump Maps, Normal Maps. | |
| Sculpting | | Sculpting is fine tuning the object's polygon mesh, or its maps. Sculpting is usually done with a (software) paint brush. | | Other Sculpting-only software includes: Mudbox®, ZBrush® (~$700). |
| Lighting & Rendering | | Lighting makes your final picture (or render) look realistic. | | Blender® (freeware) is a well known rendering "engine". |
| | | | Understanding lighting isn't trivial - you almost need a physics degree. Most mortals understand the main parameters. They then tweak and render until they get what they are looking for. | Subsurface scattering (SSS) gives more realistic looking skin.<br><br>Volumetric lighting effects are for dust particle and fog generation.<br><br>Ray tracing (which is more accurate) vs occlusion (which is faster) are different shadowing algorithms. |
| Rigging & Constraints | | Constraints are what enable you to (e.g.) drape a piece of cloth over a pedestal.<br><br>Rigging keeps the pieces of (e.g.) an animated machine moving properly with respect to one another. | Rigging is done for human (and other objects), and consists of placing rigged "bones" (or rods) inside an object. These bones are then "rigged" (or constrained) relative to each other. Each bone/rod carries a subsection of the polygon mesh of the object along with it as it moves. | You must rig before you animate.<br><br>For human meshes, the "T" position is usually the standard starting pose for rigging and/or adding bones. |
| | | Forward Kinematics (FK)<br><br>2D Planar<br>Apply IK | Our normal modo® hierarchy in the Item list is FK, e.g.:<br> thigh-> knee-> shin<br>Under the FK above, movement of the uppermost parent "root" (thigh) also moves the "goal" below it (knee and shin). | |
| | | Inverse Kinematics (IK) | thigh<-knee<-shin.<br><br>Under IK, moving the shin now affects the knee and thigh. | Modo® uses planar IK, which means it can have up to 3 items (3 item centers determine a plane) in an IK chain. Some 3D s/w packages can have more than 3 items in an IK chain (which is called multilink IK). |
| Animation | | | Is usually done on a rigged mesh. | Tweens are calculated movements between defined "key" frames. | Additional animation is done with camera movement and/or text scaling . |

Lightning Source UK Ltd.
Milton Keynes UK
UKIC01n2356260814
237586UK00006B/57